Memorable Sayings and Advices of St Philip Neri

Memorable Sayings and Advices of St PHILIP NERI

Translated out of an Italian Copy by Mr Abraham Woodhead A.M. of University College in Oxon. at the Oratory House in Hoxton. Imprinted at Oxford for Mr Obadiah Walker A.M. of the same College Anno MDCLXXXVII. Extracted from The Institutions of the Congregation of the ORATORY at St Maries in Vallicella, within the City of ROME, founded by St Philip NERIUS. Printed in Oxford, 1687, pages 56-80.

And again Imprinted at the Oxford Oratory Anno MMXII

4

Editor's Note

Abraham Woodhead (1609-78), known to his friends as the "Invisible Man", was one of the most intriguing of seventeenth-century converts. He was a fellow of University College, Oxford, before the English Civil War, and got permission to travel abroad in 1645, when he may have visited Rome. At some time in the late 1640s he became a Catholic, and he never returned to Oxford, but travelled for a time as a private tutor, before settling with some companions in a house at Hoxton, north of London. Here they lived in "pious obscurity", engaged in prayer and writing. Woodhead himself composed many works of controversy and devotion, many of which were published under a bewildering variety of coded initials by his friend Obadiah Walker, now Master of University College. Among the more uncommon of his publications was *The Institution of the Congregation of the Oratory* (1687), of which a copy was in Newman's possession at Littlemore before his conversion. That, and a few references to St Philip Neri in Woodhead's correspondence, incline one to think that the Hoxton community may have modelled itself on the Oratory.

The selection of Maxims reproduced here are not only a testimony to the piety of seventeenth-century English converts, but are still valuable for our own day, representing the spirit of St Philip, the saint "of gentleness and kindness".

See entry in the *Oxford Dictionary of National Biography* for further information and references.

The Oratory, Oxford

2006

Memorable Sayings and Advices of Saint Philip Neri

1. The Devil, who is a most proud Spirit, and a lover of darkness, is no way better conquered than by humility of heart, and by manifesting simply and clearly without any concealment all one's sins and temptations to one's Confessor.

2. According to the rules of the Fathers and ancient Monks, he that will make advancement in Religion, must dis-esteem the world, must esteem all others in it, not value himself; not value that he is not valued.

3. God evermore searcheth into the hearts of men for the spirit of humility, and a mean esteem of one's self; nor is there

anything more displeasing to him, than a swolne conceit of one's own worth.

4. When one commits a sin, or falls into some oversight; he ought presently to imagine God permitted this fall because of his pride. And surely to excuse such a defect, is a thing very dangerous; therefore who thus falls ought so often to say: *Had I been humble I had not fallen.*

5. When one is reprehended for some fault committed, he ought with all chearfulness and humility to entertain such reproof, and not to become sullen and discontent upon it; because such a pettish discontent, which out of a certain pride thinks much to be corrected, is more mischiefous than the fault it self.

6. We ought not to demand of God to visit us with afflictions and temptations out of a presumption of our own ability to conquer them; but well may we request of

him, with an humble and confident affection, grace and strength with chearfulness to undergo whatsoever he shall please to inflict.

7. When a man is afflicted by any infirmity or indisposition of Body, he ought to bethink himself seriously and say; God hath laid this weakness on me, because of something he would have to be done by, or amended in me. Therefore I resolve to change my course of life (but this by his assistance) and become a better man.

8. Fasting using of disciplines and such like other penances, ought to be done by advice of one's Confessor. For whatsoever do them of their own head, may either wrong their complexion, or may by doing them become proud, thinking themselves to have done some great matter. We must seek after knowledge, but without curiosity or anxiety; and that which we learn ought to be kept secret, making

no ostentation of it, but using it to better our life.

9. A man's heart is arrived to great perfection, when it is discreet and passeth not the limits of what is convenient. Therefore many (especially of those who begin to serve God) for want of this discretion apply themselves suddenly to a most austere life, and undertake most tiresome penances; by rigorous fastings, putting on the roughest sackcloth, lying on boards, watching and praying whole nights, when such things are disproportionate to, and much exceeding, their strength; so that in some time they remain confounded, and indisposed both in respect of body and mind.

10. We may not so apply ourselves wholly to the means, as to forget the end for which the means were used. Therefore they err exceedingly who are only intent on mortifying the body with abstinences, whippings, pilgrimages, hair cloth, or such

like, and there stay, imagining now they have done well; And know not that all this is nothing if these means do not promote us to fear God, to keep, with a love to them, his Commandments, and to humble us, and to wean us wholly from the world, that with our whole heart we may serve him.

11. Some there be who by little and little much overcharge themselves, tasking themselves to say every day their Beads, several times the hours of the blessed Virgin, the office of the Dead, and divers Prayers some for one man, some for another, and the like, all which may haply be good, but altogether are too much; and straining themselves to perform them, in the end through tediousness they give them over. Besides that so many things to be done hinder mental prayer. Therefore 'tis best to choose some good course of devotion, and so continue to practice it, and not afterward to leave it off.

12. We must not do all things in a moment, nor become saints in three or four days; but by little and little and from one degree to another.

13. There is more difficulty to remedy those who will do too much, than to incite others who do too little.

14. It is very profitable to intermit sometimes one's usual devotions, when his Confessor adviseth it. If it so fall out that his Confessor adviseth him not to communicate on his accustomed days, but defer it to another time, and the person thus advised will not obey, but is resolute still to communicate, and is displeased with what is commanded him; this is not devotion but a sign of hard-heartedness, of little mortification, and of pride, by which he is rendered most unworthy of that Sacrament.

15. When one knows how to countermand his own will, and to deny to his soul its own

desires, he is in a good degree of virtue. But not to know and not to study to do this, is to carry about one the seminary of a thousand temptations; and such a one will be apt to take offence, and to break friendship, and will seldome be cheerful, but for the most part Melancholy and troubled for the things that will befall him.

16. External devotion is no certain sign that one is truly devout, neither are tears themselves always a true sign of devotion; because ill women easily weep, yet are no Saints for it.

17. If from any person one receives a repulse, he ought by no means to take it ill, or shew sign of discontent, but continue towards them the same cheerful countenance, as formerly, and to take from them all suspition of his small satisfaction.

18. When it is needful to admonish any person of quality of some notable defect, the

best way is to let the reprehension fall on some third person, for so they will more easily and gently take it to themselves; and not be angry that one should dare to play the Master over them.

19. Who would be much obeyed, let him not command too much.

20. Then the obedience is good when one obeys without arguing, and holds it for a rule, that what is commanded is fittest to be done. And whoso enters into a Society ought to be most ready to obey; and to leave all private, for the common, affairs.

21. It is not enough only to honor our Superiors, but we ought also to honor our equals and our inferiors, and to strive to be the first in giving honor.

22. It is a thing appertaining to virtue to fly all manner of singularity, and not to make shew to be, or to do, anything more than others.

23. Raptures, Extasies, and tears in publick and in the sight of people, are suspicious; because Grace loves the recess and privacy of the heart, except so far as it is necessary to manifest it for the good of our neighbour; and Nature seeks her own, and loves to make an outward shew and appearance.

24. We ought not to delay to do well, for death delays not to approach; and happy is the young man to whom God gives time to be able to do good.

25. Idleness is a pestilence to a Christian; and therefore must we always be doing something, especially when alone in our chamber; either reading some book of Devotion, or the lives of the Saints, or the H. Scripture; or saying our Prayers, or ordering our books, or making our bed, or some such thing that the devil may never find us idle.

26. To go on in the way of virtue it is a good motive to consider, that in this world there is no Purgatory for us, but either Paradise or Hell; because he who serves God as he ought all labour and infirmity turns to his consolation, and he hath within himself a Paradise; but he who doth the contrary, and giveth himself to sensuality, hath Hell in this world, and in the next.

27. The frequent Confession of sins brings great good to our soul; for it purifies, and heals, and confirms it in God's service. Therefore our set time to perform it must not be deferred for any business whatsoever which may then occur; but first we ought to go to confession, and afterward about our affairs, in which we may hope for the better success by this help.

28. Melancholy and trouble of mind brings great hurt to the spirit, whereas chearfulness fortifies the heart, and makes

one persevere the better in a good life. Therefore the servant of God ought always to be cheerful.

29. Scruples, because they disquiet the mind and make it melancholick, ought to be greatly shunned.

30. We must not ask of God temporal blessings, as health, riches, prosperity, and the like, absolutely, but conditionally; if it please God, and if they be expedient.

31. When God bestows on us any internal grace we ought not to disclose it except to our spiritual Father, other wise we loose it.

32. Who goeth to serve the sick, or do other charities, must imagin such a sick person to be Christ, and all he doeth to him to be done to Christ him self; for so it is done with more love and benefit.

33. When any man doth a good work, and another ascribes it to him self, and assumes the glory of it, he who did it ought exceedingly to rejoice, and acknowledge it as a great favour from God, that others take that from him before men, because he shall recover it with greater reward before God.

34. He doth ill who hath confidence of him self; and he who puts himself on the occasion of a sin, saying, I shall not fall, commonly doth fall with greater damage of his own soul; who would not fall let him not trust to him self, nor presume on his own strength; but say to God, *Lord trust not to me, nor expect any thing else of me but evil*; and *I shall assuredly fall if thou help me not.*

35. To keep far off all danger of impurity young men ought to fly carefully whatsoever (even the smallest) occasion of this sin. Therefore this Holy man forbad his

spiritual children to touch one another
not so much as by the hands, although but
in jesting.

36. When the soul resigns it self into the
hands of God, and is contented with the
divine good pleasure, it remains in good
hands, and is very secure that it will go
well with it; and it belongs especially to
a sick man to resign over himself, and to
say to God, *Lord, if thou wilt have me, be-*
hold here I am; tho I have done no good at all,
do with me what seems good to thee.

37. Who willeth anything but Christ,
knoweth not what he would have; who
asketh any thing but Christ, knoweth not
what he asketh; who worketh and not for
Christ, knoweth not what he doth.

38. We must not be fastned to any thing in
this world, be it never so small a matter:
but we must be humbly affected amongst
the creatures, and desire to have so low

a condition as to stand in need of Six-
pence, and, begging for it, to be denied
it.

39. Who would have riches shall never have
the Spirit.

40. The soul who gives it self to God must be
wholly God's; and what love is bestowed
on Parents and kindred, or on studies, or
on it self, of so much love is God deprived.

41. The man who loves God with true love,
and prizeth him above all things, sometimes in his prayers meets with an over-
flowing of tears, and a concours of graces,
or feelings of the Spirit, in such abun-
dance that he is forced to beg in abate-
ment.

42. One ought to reserve for himself neither
place, nor time, when there is need to help
his neighbour; and ought to quit his Spiritual gusts and his prayers for his neighbour, and leave Christ for Christ. And

this is a great perfection, and few know how to do it.

43. When God's servant hath no troubles, nor any to persecute him and treat him injuriously; if he would find the Spirit, let him imagin that some wicked man comes to affront him, and sayeth much villany against him, and to injurious words addeth as uncivil deeds, beats him with a cudgel, or wounds him with a sword, and with his fist makes his face black and blew; and being this abused, then with great fervency of love in imitation of Christ let him incline his heart to pardon the wrong that is done him, and overcoming all angry motions that may arise, and not willing for the love of God to take any revenge let him with great love forgive him, as if he had truly received such an injury; that by the frequent practice of such imaginations the heart may accustom itself to pardon a real injury; as the souldier who learns to play at foils, by accustom-

ing him self to handle his armes afterwards makes use of his art to fight in good
earnest.

44. Suffering Penance is still necessary to the
servant of God; and when straightned
with any affliction, then let him expect
a Consolation: for God never sends an
affliction, but that he sends after it a consolation: and in summe, the whole life
of him, who serves God, is nothing else
but first a consolation, and then another
trouble.

45. When God visits any man with an affliction, and he hath not patience to bear it,
it may be well said unto him: *Thou art
not worthy of God's visitation, nor deservest so
great a benefit.*

46. When there come against us tribulations,
infirmities, and things much contrary to
us, we are not timorously to fly them, but
valiantly to overcome them; because if

thou fly from any of them, another worse will come upon thee: who flies from a hoar-frost will be covered with snow; who flies from a Bear meets with a Lion.

47. When God's servant goeth to receive in the Sacrament the glorious Body of Christ, in which are all the delights of heaven, he ought to stand in fear, and prepare himself more than ordinarily for future temptations; because the marvellous Graces, which are conferred in that divine Sacrament, God will not have to lie idle; for Grace more abhors idleness, than Nature doth vacuities.

48. When anyone feels within his heart a new and extraordinary spirit, for the reason before mentioned let him stand prepared for some temptation and tribulation; and whilst one feels in him this ardour of the Spirit, let him ask of God strength to be able to endure whatsoever from heaven he shall be ordained to suffer, and that

the temptation induce him not to any sins, great, or little.

49. If any should ask, what is the greatest tribulation a true servant of God can have? It may be answered him, Not to have any tribulation at all.

50. Let young men beware of the sin of the flesh, and old men of the sin of avarice; the first is overcome by flying, the second by resisting.

51. A man must always stand in fear, and not trust to himself, because the Devil makes his assault unexpected, and darkens the understanding; and who stands not in fear is overcome, because self-confident he is destitute of the help of God.

52. In the temptations which the lasciviousness of the flesh suggests to us let the tempted have recourse instantly to God, and make thrice on his heart the sign of

the H. Cross, and say: *Christ, thou Son of God, have mercy on me* or the verse of the Psalm, *O God make speed to save me, O Lord make hast to help me*; or this *Create in me a clean heart O God, and renew right spirit within me*; and let him kiss the earth, and say to the tempter, *I will accuse thee to my spiritual Father if thou temptest me any more.*

53. Obedience against our inclinations is to be practised in small matters, and which seem of no consequence; because thus we attain a facility to yield it in greater.

54. The mortification of the will and understanding in matter of obedience to Superiors is much more beneficial, and attains sooner to perfection, than great corporal Penances.

55. It is not sufficient to consider, if God will have such good done as is attempted, but if he will have it done by our means, in such a manner, at such a time: which appearing, not to be God's will, we ought

contentedly to desist from any such en-
terprise.

56. There is nothing better for man than
Prayer, and without it he cannot endure
long in the way of the Spirit; therefore
every moment must he have recourse to
this most powerful means of Salvation.

57. The enemy of our salvation fears nothing
more, nothing makes him sadder, nothing he seeks more to hinder, than Prayer.

58. When one is praying, let not his bodily
eyes be so fixed on an Image that he never
removes them from it, for this will hurt
the Head; but let him make use of an Image for the help of his memory: as, for example, to reduce into his mind the benefit of the Incarnation of Christ, or his
Nativity, or his death on the Cross; or if
it be the Image of a holy man, or a holy
woman, let him make use of it to put him

in mind of their virtues, that he may imitate them, and pray them to intercede for God for him.

59. To know how to pray well, it is a very great help to read the Lives of the Saints, and when the Spirit inclines him to meditate on them; and so when it inclines to think on the passion of Christ then to follow that attraction; and not to pray or meditate differently from that to which the Spirit moves.

60. Fancies, which intervene, are a great disturbance to prayer; and many troubled with such by-thoughts give it over: but they do not well; for, notwithstanding any such fancies, one ought to persevere still, as much as may be, in prayer; and God often gives in a moment that which could not be obtained in a long time.

61. Amongst other things, we are to ask of God, a chief is perseverance in well-doing, and well-serving of God; because

if any hath patience and perseverance in well-doing in a good life after once begun, he will acquire an exceeding great measure of Spirit.

62. In the beginning of the conversion of a soul to God the Spirit useth to come sometimes strongly upon him; but afterwards it seems as it were to go away, and the Lord shews thereby as if he had forsaken him; but stand he firm, and it will return again.

63. God useth almost never to send death to one who much serves him, but that he first notifies it to him by some sign, or by giving him the Spirit extraordinarily.

64. There are three degrees in a Spiritual life: the first is called an animal life; the second the life of a man; the third the life of an Angel; that is to say, the Lord useth in the beginning, for the drawing of souls

to himself, to entice them with sweetnes, and with a certain spirit and gusts extraordinary, and then afterward he makes a shew to go far from them, withdrawing his most holy hand from these sweet treatments, to see if they stand firm in the Spirit, leaving them to fight it out for a little time; and then when they have made resistance for a while, and have overcome those tribulations and temptations he restores afterwards their heavenly gusts and consolations doubled; and this is a life Angelical, void of all pain or offence.

65. It is no pride to desire to exceed in sanctity any Saint whatsoever; because to desire to be a Saint is to desire we may have the will to love and to honour God above all things: and this desire, if it were possible, ought to be extended to infinity, because God is worthy of infinite love, and because his greatness is infinite.

66. No man ought ever to trust his own prudence, but in all things to ask counsel of

God, consult his Confessor, and beg the prayers of others.

67. To maintain our selves in a good life, and the holy service of God, frequent Confession and the holy Communion are most necessary; for the right practising of these is a very great help.

68. For Graces obtained by the way of prayer we must continue so long our prayer till the grace be perfected; and if prayer be intermitted God doth sometimes suspend the grace. Therefore is a sick man, for whom prayer is made, begin to mend upon the prayers made for him, then these must not be ceased; but as such recovery as begun by prayer, even so by the strength of prayer must it be perfected.

69. When he, who prayeth, feels in the continuation of his prayer great quietness of spirit, it is a good sign, that God either hath or will grant the grace he sues for.

70. Many feeling within themselves carnal temptations or the like, doubt sometimes whether they have consented or no; but if the person tempted feel in himself still a love toward that virtue against which he was tempted, and a hatred against that vice; it is a sign he hath not consented. Likewise if he would not swear that he hath consented, it is a sign that he hath not consented; because when there is a deliberate consent the soul easily perceives it.

71. After the temptation past we must not reason if we have consented or not; for such reasonings cause a return of carnal temptations.

72. Carnal temptations ought to be feared and fled even in sickness and in old age itself, so long as we are able to shut and open our eyes; for the spirit of fornication spares neither time nor person.

73. The servant of God, if with more security he will walk amongst so many snares spread abroad in all places, let him have for an intercessor for him to her Son the Bl. Virgin.

74. Church-goods must be employed sparingly, and not be spent but upon necessity, because they are goods which belong to God.

75. Chearfulness and mirth is good in him who serves God, but he must flie dissoluteness, and be careful not to fall into a spirit of jesting; for they who delight in jesting render themselves incapable of ever receiving the Spirit of God, and if they have any thing that is good in them, they lose it suddenly.

76. When the Priest visits the sick let him not play the Prophet, saying, that the sick person will not recover; because sometimes having prophesied death, if the sick

become well again he is displeased that he
hath erred in his prophecy.

77. A Confessor is to be chosen with seri-
ous deliberation, for it is a great advan-
tage to have a good guide in so diffi-
cult a way; but having chosen one he is
not easily to be changed, but to be be-
lieved and conferred-with about our oc-
currences, because God will never per-
mit that a Confessor should err in a thing
that might be a hinderance to the soul of
a Penitent.

78. To profit by reading the lives of Saints, or
other Spiritual books, we must not read
them with curiosity, or in hast, but by little and little; and when any feels himself
touched, or that some devotion ariseth
in him, he must go no further, but shut
the book and there stop, and hearken to
the Spirit; and when it fails, return to his
Reading.

79. To pray well the soul must first bring it self into a most profound humility, and know it self unworthy to stand before so great a Majesty, and to shew to God its necessities and its weakness, and being humbled cast it self on God, that he may teach it to pray.

80. When any man remains listless and all-discontented, or feels his sensual appetite troublesom and frequent, he must not lose courage: because when God will bestow any virtue, he permits a temptation of the contrary vice; that by fighting and resisting a man may make himself capable of that virtue, against which he was assaulted.

81. It is not fitting to leave off doing any good work because one feels some rising of vain-glory; because as often as vain-glory is not the Mistress but a companion of the work, it takes not away the worth of the work, the perfection is in this that it be a servant.

82. Whosoever desires to live in a strict way of Religion, let him first learn to subdue his will in some thing, wherein he finds greatest opposition, because thus with more facility he shall persevere.

83. When anyone of his own accord would fast, use discipline, wear sack-cloth; or the like, and his Confessor doth not like it; the Confessor ought not to be violently urged to give any such licence.

84. Let a man stay in his own house, *i.e.* within himself, and not become a *Syndick*, or judge of the actions and lives of others; if he desires not to make rash judgments, nor to murmur at, nor to despise, his neighbour.

85. A young Convert is not to seek to convert others, but to be careful to confirm himself, and to make himself strong against temptations, and to be humble, and not to think he hath done any great matter,

but rather to esteem himself to have done nothing, that he fall not into pride.

86. Scrupulous persons are in all things, whatsoever to depend upon their spiritual Father, and not trust their own judgment; otherwise they will never be able to deliver themselves; they may well find a truce, but not a peace.

87. A man, who serves God, must remain resigned to feel the gusts of the things of God, and to want them; to entertain chearfulness and sadness.

88. It is a thing very dangerous to spiritual persons to desire to see visions; and many, who have followed after such a spirit, have fallen into great ruine.

89. To cure any one, who hath fallen into some sin after a virtuous life led for a long time, there is no greater means to reduce him to his first condition, than to

make him do some eminent mortification; that is to make him discover his fault to some others of a singular good life, with whom he hath some intimacy, in whom he may confide; because by such humility God will raise him up to his former estate again.

90. All men are much concerned in the quiet of their own conscience; therefore if any would make some particular vow, the Holy Man thought it good for the most part that it should be made conditional; as thus *If I can*; *If I remember*, or in some such manner.

91. In everything and for everything we ought to throw our selves into the hands of our Lord: for if God will have us to do nothing more than we do, yet he will make us good in that which we do.

92. A Religious man, who is in an Order fallen away from its ancient discipline,

and findeth in himself great gifts of the spirit, ought not to leave his own Order, to enter into another, but to abide therein: for God will make use of him towards the reforming of his Order by his good Example.

93. We must not be swift in advising our brother concerning his defects and wants; but first we are to consider our selves, afterwards others; and to do it with much prudence.

94. Every man ought to live so holily every day, and to frame all his actions in such a manner, as if that should be his last day.

95. If thou lovest all men with true love, thou canst never bear hatred to any man; neither for words spoken against thee, nor for dis-curtesies received; for in a heart, where there is not love to our neighbour whomever, there God is not.

96. Who perceives some discontentedness in him self ought not to be troubled at it; for it will quickly pass over; but in the mean-time to overcome such an ill passion he must say his prayers, or sing some spiritual Hymn of praise.

97. We must be ready to obey the will of our Superiors, and to do rather the will of another than our own.

98. Whosoever desires that Christ should give him the first place in heaven, let him be well pleased to stand always in the last place here on earth; and when any one perceives him self despised let him thank God for it, hoping that honor is reserved for him in heaven.

99. Let all things be taken in good part, and judge not other mens actions; but learn to have compassion on our neighbours defects; thinking with our selves, that if God did not hold his hand upon our head

we should do worse: and he who hath any good parts let him not be proud, but give thanks to God, from whom cometh every good.

100. We must seek Christ where he is not, *i.e.* in Crosses and Tribulations, where now our Redeemer, who is crowned with glory, is not to be found; and when any falls into Tribulations, he must not complain; because they are sent from God our most loving Father and most merciful Lord, to procure us the greater crown in heaven.

101. Every day for some short time read some spiritual book, and be careful to retain in memory some particular point which may be profitable to your soul.

102. When there is occasion to buy anything none ought to be moved with affection to it, but with the need or want of it; and the holy Man used on such occasions to say: *I buy not affections.*

103. At the time of receiving the Holy Communion we should beg a remedy against that vice we find ourselves most inclined to.

104. When anyone visits the Altars let him ask from the Saints of these Altars a spiritual Alms; this being a good way to acquire the Spirit and Devotion.